W9-BLM-801

Today's Superst★rs
Entertainment

Miley Cyrus
Hannah Montana

By Jennifer Magid

Gareth Stevens
Publishing

Please visit our web site at www.garethstevens.com.
For a free color catalog describing our list of high-quality books,
call 1-800-542-2595 (USA) or 1-800-387-3178 (Canada). Our fax: 1-877-542-2596

Library of Congress Cataloging-in-Publication Data
Magid, Jennifer.
  Miley Cyrus/Hannah Montana / by Jennifer Magid.
      p. cm. — (Today's superstars. Entertainment)
    Includes bibliographical references and index.
    ISBN-13: 978-0-8368-9236-9 (lib. bdg.)
    ISBN-10: 0-8368-9236-4 (lib. bdg.)
    1. Cyrus, Miley, 1992—Juvenile literature. 2. Television actors and
    actresses—United States—Juvenile literature. 3. Hannah Montana
    (Television program)—Juvenile literature. I. Title.
  ML3930.C98M35   2008
  782.42164092—dc22 [B]   2008020733

This edition first published in 2009 by
Gareth Stevens Publishing
A Weekly Reader® Company
1 Reader's Digest Road
Pleasantville, NY 10570-7000 USA

Senior Managing Editor: Lisa M. Herrington
Senior Editor: Brian Fitzgerald
Creative Director: Lisa Donovan
Senior Designer: Keith Plechaty
Production Designer: Cynthia Malaran
Photo Researcher: Kim Babbitt

Photo credits: cover Jason DeCrow/AP Images, title page, p. 7 Disney Channel;
p. 5 Charley Gallay/Getty Images; p. 9 WireImage/Getty Images; p. 10 Ron
Galella/Getty Images; p. 13 Bob D'Amico/Disney Channel; p. 15 Jesse Grant/
Getty Images; p. 17 Jeffrey Mayer/Getty Images; p. 18 Joel Warren/Disney
Channel; p. 19 Byron Cohen/Disney Channel; p. 20 Frazer Harrison/Getty
Images; p. 21 Jennifer Graylock/AP Images; p. 22 Adam Larkey/Disney Channel;
p. 24 Disney Channel; p. 25 Adam Larkey/Disney Channel; p. 26 Michael
Loccisano/FilmMagic/Getty Images; p. 28 Adam Larkey/Disney Channel.

Printed in the United States

2 3 4 5 6 7 8 9 10 09 08

Contents

Words in the glossary appear in **bold** type the first time they are used in the text.

Chapter 1

The Best of Both Worlds

In January 2008, a buzz was building outside El Capitan Theatre in Hollywood, California. The streets surrounding the theater were closed. Traffic was at a standstill. Thousands of people lined the sidewalks. They were waiting to see their favorite star, Miley Cyrus. The 15-year-old actress and singer was in town for a special reason. Her movie *Hannah Montana & Miley Cyrus: Best of Both Worlds Concert* was about to open.

Fans and photographers screamed Miley's name as she walked down the red carpet. Cameras flashed all around her. "I'm so excited to be here," she told *People* magazine. "It's the first time I've ever been at my own **premiere**."

Miley posed for photographers at the *Best of Both Worlds* premiere.

Being Number One

Miley would soon have another reason to be excited. Her movie opened at number one. It was shown in fewer theaters than most new movies. Yet it made $31 million in its first week. The movie gave fans a behind-the-scenes look at Miley's live shows. Her record-breaking Best of Both Worlds Tour wrapped up just before the movie came out.

On Top of the World

The tour and movie capped off an amazing run for Miley. Both of her albums had been number-one hits. The TV show that started it all, *Hannah Montana*, was the most popular show on cable. More than 3 million viewers tuned in to each episode.

Miley has conquered television, music, and movies. Yet in many ways, she is a lot like her character on *Hannah Montana*. She's part world-famous superstar and part normal teenager. "I still have to do school, and I still make time to hang out with my friends," she said on *The Oprah Winfrey Show*. "Because that's what's most important."

Just a few years ago, Miley was an unknown kid from Tennessee. She faced the same rejection that most young actors do. In fact, she almost didn't get the role on *Hannah Montana*. During her amazing rise to stardom, Miley's secret to success has remained the same. "You have to keep believing in yourself," she says.

Fact File

In 2008, *Time* magazine named Miley one of the 100 Most Influential People in the World. It was the second straight year she made the list. Oprah Winfrey and President George W. Bush were just two of the other big names on the list.

Fans got to see Miley up close in her 3-D concert movie.

3-D on the Screen

Thousands of fans couldn't get tickets to Miley's sold-out concerts. The movie *Hannah Montana & Miley Cyrus: Best of Both Worlds Concert* gave them a chance to see what they had missed. The movie was released in 3-D. At a 3-D movie, viewers wear special glasses. The glasses make them feel as if the characters are in the theater, not just on the screen.

Miley's concert movie shows what it's like to be on tour with her. "This is, like, better than front row," she told the Associated Press. "You could reach out and feel like you can touch my hand."

Chapter 2
Growing Up Cyrus

Destiny Hope Cyrus was born on November 23, 1992 in Nashville, Tennessee. "My dad named me Destiny Hope because he said my destiny was to bring hope," Miley told interviewer Barbara Walters. Destiny's parents, Billy Ray and Tish, gave her an unusual nickname when she was a baby. They called her "Smiley" because she always had a grin. Her nickname was soon shortened to Miley.

Billy Ray Cyrus was at the top of the music world when Miley was born. He was a popular country singer. He decided that family was most important, though. Billy Ray soon stopped touring and settled his family in Tennessee.

Fact File

Miley legally changed her name to Miley Ray Cyrus in 2008. She added "Ray" to honor her dad, Billy Ray Cyrus.

Miley's parents, her sister Noah, and her brother Braison joined her at the premiere of *High School Musical 2.*

Full House

Miley was raised on a 500-acre farm near Nashville. Her home was always very busy. She grew up with five brothers and sisters. The Cyrus family had a lot of pets, including seven horses!

Miley loved to perform from a young age. "When I was little, I would stand up on couches and say, 'Watch me,' " Miley told BMI.com. "We had these showers that are completely glass," she recalled. "I would lock people in them and make them stay in there and watch me perform."

Billy Ray played with baby Miley before a 1994 concert.

Billy Ray's Achy Breaky Heart

Many fans know Billy Ray Cyrus as Miley's dad and costar. In the early 1990s, however, he was almost as popular as Miley is today. "Everywhere we went when I was young, girls would go crazy over my dad," Miley told the *Daily Mail*. Billy Ray's country dance hit "Achy Breaky Heart" was the top song of 1992. The top albums today sell about 3 million copies. Sales of Billy Ray's album *Some Gave All* passed 9 million! Billy Ray recorded more country albums in the 1990s. He could not repeat the success of "Achy Breaky Heart," however.

He later turned to acting. He starred in the TV show *Doc* from 2001 to 2004. He played a country doctor living in New York. Billy Ray's success has had a big impact on Miley. "I grew up learning from my dad," she told an Australian newspaper. "He's the reason I'm doing what I do."

What's Up, Doc?

Miley got her first acting job because of her dad. In 2001, Billy Ray got the lead role in the TV series *Doc*. The show filmed in Toronto, Canada. Billy Ray was away from his family for weeks at a time. Miley would visit him on the set. In 2003, Billy Ray helped Miley get a small role in an episode.

Big Fish, Small Role

Miley also made her movie **debut** that year. She won the role of Ruthie in the film *Big Fish*. Her character's big scene is spying on a witch with a group of other children. Miley's part in the movie was small, but she had a lot of fun. She decided to **audition** for other acting jobs.

Facing Rejection

Getting acting jobs wasn't easy. Billy Ray watched Miley get rejected for one part after another. He knew that acting was a tough business. "He didn't want to see his little girl get hurt," Miley told Barbara Walters. "But every time I got knocked down, I wanted to get back up again." All her hard work would soon pay off.

Fact File

Miley's younger sister Noah is also an actress. She appeared in episodes of *Doc* and *Hannah Montana*.

Chapter 3 Introducing Hannah Montana

When Miley was 11, she auditioned for a new Disney Channel series. She tried out for two roles. One was a teen who leads a secret life as a pop star. The other was the role of the girl's best friend, Lilly. Miley didn't get either part. The **producers** thought she was too small and too young.

Disney continued to search for the right lead actress. But Miley wouldn't let them forget about her. She kept sending the producers videotapes of herself performing. Finally, a year later, they called Miley in for another audition.

"She stood in front of us and knocked us out," said Gary Marsh, the Disney Channel entertainment president. Miley was finally offered the lead role of Hannah Montana.

Best of the Rest

The rest of the cast still had to be picked. After Miley got the role, Billy Ray got a phone call. The producers wanted him to play Miley's father on the show! Billy Ray was a natural for the part. "It was just pretty obvious the chemistry between Miley and me is just so real," he told CNN.

Emily Osment was cast as Lilly Truscott, Miley's best friend. Mitchel Musso got the part of Miley's other good friend, Oliver. Jason Earles won the role of Miley's goofy older brother, Jackson.

Fact File

Like Miley, Emily Osment has been acting since she was very young. Emily played Gerti Giggles in the *Spy Kids* movies. Her older brother Haley Joel appeared in *Forrest Gump* and *The Sixth Sense*.

The *Hannah Montana* cast (from left): Emily Osment, Miley Cyrus, Jason Earles (standing), Billy Ray Cyrus, and Mitchel Musso.

Taking Control

On *Hannah Montana*, Miley plays a character named Miley Stewart. By day, Miley Stewart is an ordinary girl. She deals with school, friends, and her annoying brother! At night, she puts on a blond wig and becomes pop star Hannah Montana. The character's dad, Robby Stewart, is also her manager. Miley has to keep her double life a secret.

Getting into her new role was easy for Miley. In a lot of ways, *Hannah Montana* was like her real life! Her character's name is Miley, and her real dad plays her dad on TV. On the show, the Stewarts moved from Tennessee to California. In real life, the Cyrus family also had to move to California for Miley's new job.

Hanging With Dad

Imagine if you had to go to work with your dad every day. That's life for Miley and Billy Ray. How do they do it? "We're really close," Miley told *People* magazine. "When we come home, we forget that we even work together, and just hang out."

Billy Ray agrees. "I'm just having a lot of fun getting to act with my little girl and be her daddy and be her best friend," he told *People*.

Emily Osment and Miley are great friends. Miley told *Teen* magazine, "We love each other like sisters."

Spreading the Word

Hannah Montana premiered on March 24, 2006. In the episode, Miley tells Lilly that she is secretly Hannah Montana. The show was an instant hit. More than 5 million people watched the first episode. *Hannah Montana* quickly became the most-watched kids' show on cable television.

The show's success was only the beginning for Miley. Her real life would soon get just as wild as Hannah's. She was about to become a pop star herself.

Fact File

Corbin Bleu played Miley's classmate Johnny in the first episode of *Hannah Montana*. Disney fans know him as Chad from *High School Musical*.

Chapter 4
Miley Mania

Hannah Montana was a big hit. Disney wanted to build on the show's popularity. Miley began to perform in public as Hannah Montana. Her first concert was in June 2006. It took place at Typhoon Lagoon at Walt Disney World in Orlando, Florida. Miley loved being onstage. "All the fans just went wild for everything," she said. "It was awesome." The concert later aired on the Disney Channel.

On Tour

Later that year, Miley got her first chance to tour. She was the opening act for fellow Disney stars the Cheetah Girls. Miley played 20 dates across the country. Fans were excited to see Hannah Montana live. Soon, they would make Miley one of the biggest stars in music.

Miley's Music

Disney released the *Hannah Montana* sound track on October 24, 2006. The album included eight songs that Miley performed as Hannah Montana. The album also included "I Learned From You," a **duet** by Miley and her dad.

The *Hannah Montana* sound track was number one on the **music chart** for two weeks. It went on to sell more than 3 million copies. Music **critics** liked Miley's singing, too. They said she sounded very mature for a 13-year-old.

Fact File

In July 2006, Miley appeared in a special Disney episode called "That's So Suite Life of Hannah Montana." It brought together three popular shows: *The Suite Life of Zack and Cody, That's So Raven,* and *Hannah Montana.*

Miley performed as Hannah Montana during her 2006 tour. The show's theme, "The Best of Both Worlds," was a crowd favorite.

Hannah Stays Hot

Meanwhile, *Hannah Montana* was still going strong on the Disney Channel. Miley's character even got a chance for a little romance. She began dating actor Jake Ryan, played by Cody Linley. Miley had her first on-screen kiss with Cody. "It was, like, the best 10 seconds of my life," she told *Teen* magazine.

Season two of *Hannah Montana* began in a big way on April 23, 2007. Five new episodes aired on five straight nights! The season was packed with famous guest stars. Jesse McCartney, Dwayne "The Rock" Johnson, and Joey Fatone were just a few of them.

In season two of *Hannah Montana*, Miley and Jake (played Cody Linley) decided to just be good friends.

Dolly Parton says that Miley is a "fantastic singer and songwriter."

Hello, Dolly!

One of the biggest stars to appear on *Hannah Montana* is Dolly Parton. She plays Miley Stewart's godmother, who is also named Dolly. The role is easy for Dolly to play. Dolly Parton is Miley Cyrus's real-life godmother!

Dolly is a legend in country music. She started her singing career in Nashville when she was not much older than Miley. She wrote and sang "I Will Always Love You" and many other classic songs. Dolly has also had a successful career as an actress.

Dolly says that Miley has a bright future. "I think that she's gonna have a big career," Dolly told AOL Music. "I'm amazed at the talent that child has and the effect she has on people."

Center of Attention

Miley's fast rise to stardom has a downside. She can no longer do a lot of things that most teenagers do. She loves to shop, but she can't go to a mall without being surrounded by fans. "It's insane," she told *USA Today*. "Managers and everyone hate me. They're like, 'Please get out of the store,' because it gets so insane. It's pretty crazy, how fast it all came."

Award Winner

Miley had a hit TV show and a hit album. In 2007, she began to pile up awards, too. In March, she won a Kids' Choice Award for favorite television actress. The award was special because kids vote for the winners. In August, Miley won a Teen Choice Award for best TV actress in a comedy. The award was a surfboard! *Hannah Montana* was named the best TV comedy.

Miley showed off her 2007 Teen Choice Award.

Dressed for Success

It's hard for Miley to go anywhere without seeing her own face! There are Miley toothbrushes, Halloween costumes, dolls, and video games. Disney also released the popular Hannah Montana clothing line in summer 2007.

"When I was in Nashville, I went to our Macy's and went and tried on all the Hannah Montana stuff. Then I said, 'This is weird. I'm wearing my face,' " Miley told *USA Today*.

On *Hannah Montana*, Miley is careful to pick clothes that are right for a girl her age. "I say what I'm comfortable in ... nothing that's too out there," she told Oprah Winfrey. "I like to look kind of like what girls would want to look up to."

Miley introduced the Hannah Montana clothing line in June 2007.

Back on Top

On June 26, 2007, *Hannah Montana 2: Meet Miley Cyrus* hit music stores. It was a double album. The first CD included more songs from *Hannah Montana* episodes. Miley sang all the songs, but Hannah Montana was listed as the artist. The second CD was Miley's first album as herself. She cowrote eight of the 10 songs.

Hannah Montana 2: Meet Miley Cyrus shot to number one in its first week. It outsold the first *Hannah Montana* album. Miley made music history. She became the youngest artist to have two number-one albums in less than a year. Miley's upbeat dance tune "See You Again" became her first top 10 single.

Next up was Miley's first concert tour as the main act. Miley mania was about to reach a new level.

Miley had a very small role in *High School Musical 2*. She danced by the pool during the final song. She was on-screen for only two seconds!

Chapter 5

Happy to Be Hannah

In October 2007, Miley began a 54-date concert tour. It was called the Best of Both Worlds Tour. Miley performed both as herself and Hannah Montana. Fans couldn't wait to see Miley live. They were also excited to see her opening act, the Jonas Brothers. Across the country, tickets sold out almost instantly. More than 12,000 seats sold out in eight minutes in Memphis, Tennessee. Her show near Atlanta, Georgia, sold out in just four minutes!

Every night, Miley was singing for packed arenas. She felt a lot of pressure to be at her best for her fans. "Sometimes, it's like, wow, I really have to be good," she told CNN. "This is their one chance to see the show, and it's the one night I'm going to be here, so it has to be perfect."

Birthday Wish

Miley had a great time on tour. One of the most special moments came on November 23. Miley celebrated her 15th birthday with a concert in her hometown of Nashville. The crowd of 15,000 fans sang "Happy Birthday." Miley told the crowd that her one birthday wish was to be in her hometown with her fans. "Anyone from a small town can go out there and live their dream," she said. "So to be here with you guys tonight on my birthday is amazing."

On tour, Miley showed her skills as a guitarist. She ended many shows by playing "I Miss You." She wrote the song about her grandfather, who died two years earlier.

The Jonas Brothers (from left): Nick, Joe, and Kevin.

Oh, Brothers!

The Best of Both Worlds Tour featured another top young act. The Jonas Brothers are almost as popular as Miley. Their songs "S.O.S." and "When You Look Me in the Eyes" became big hits for the trio.

The brothers appeared on *Hannah Montana* on August 18, 2007. In the episode, Miley gets jealous when her dad starts writing songs for the Jonas Brothers. The episode got one of the highest ratings in cable TV history. Nearly 11 million people tuned in!

In June 2008, the Jonas Brothers starred in the hit Disney Channel movie *Camp Rock*. They played a music group called Connect 3. **Tabloids** spread rumors that Miley and Nick Jonas were dating. She said they are just really good friends.

More of a Good Thing

The Best of Both Worlds Tour was a huge success. Miley and her managers decided to keep it going. They added 14 more shows. The tour ended on January 31, 2008, in Miami, Florida.

The next day, the 3-D movie *Hannah Montana & Miley Cyrus: Best of Both Worlds Concert* premiered across the country. It was the number-one movie that week. Disney decided to let it run longer. They wanted to let as many fans see the movie as possible.

Miley and Ashley Tisdale appeared together on MTV's *Total Request Live* in June 2006.

Famous Friends

Miley says that one of the hardest parts of touring is being away from her friends. She is very close with her costars Emily Osment and Mitchel Musso. She is also good friends with other Disney stars. "All my friends are on the Disney Channel," she told Oprah Winfrey, "because they're the only people I get to hang out with all the time."

One of her closest friends is Ashley Tisdale. She plays Maddie on *The Suite Life of Zack and Cody* and Sharpay in *High School Musical.* "Every time that I'm home when I want to go see her, she's working, too," Miley says. "So I miss her a lot."

Giving Back

Miley is very busy, but she finds time to help others. She often visits sick children in hospitals. She also donated $1 from each ticket sold during her concert tour to the City of Hope. The organization treats cancer patients and is working to find a cure. Cancer research is an important cause for Miley. Her grandfather died of cancer not long before she became famous.

Popular Choice

In March 2008, Miley won two more Kids' Choice Awards. She was named favorite TV actress and favorite female singer. She also performed "G.N.O. (Girls Night Out)" during the show. In May, Miley and the *Hannah Montana* cast starting filming a movie. The film is set in Miley's hometown of Nashville.

Under Pressure

Miley knows she is a role model for thousands of kids. She takes that responsibility seriously. Miley says she has faced the same pressures as other young stars. So far, she has avoided going out to parties and doing things that could get her into trouble. "You don't have to fall into what everyone else is doing," she told Oprah Winfrey. "I just have to say, 'Be true to yourself. Be a kid. Grow up slowly.' "

Fact File

Miley goes to school, but not like most other kids do. On set or on tour, she has a tutor for three hours each morning.

No matter what she does next, Miley will always make time for her fans.

Future Plans

What is next for Miley? Will she stick with acting or focus on music? "It depends, because acting is so cool," she told MTV. "But singing is a better way to be yourself, so I can't choose."

Miley really isn't worried about what she will do next. She is happy to see where life takes her. "What I decided before I came out to L.A. and started working, was the minute I didn't have fun was the minute I go home," Miley told *People*. Her fans hope she will stick around for many years to come.

☆ Time Line

1992   Destiny Hope Cyrus is born on November 23, in Nashville, Tennessee.

2003   Makes her first TV appearance on her father's show *Doc*; plays Ruthie in the movie *Big Fish*.

2006   Stars in the new Disney Channel series *Hannah Montana*; tours with the Cheetah Girls; the *Hannah Montana* sound track hits number one.

2007   Wins a Kids' Choice Award and a Teen Choice Award; season two of *Hannah Montana* premieres; the double album *Hannah Montana 2: Meet Miley Cyrus* is a number-one hit; launches the Best of Both Worlds Tour.

2008   Stars in the hit 3-D movie *Hannah Montana & Miley Cyrus: Best of Both Worlds Concert*; legally changes her name to Miley Ray Cyrus; wins two more Kids' Choice Awards; starts filming the *Hannah Montana* movie.

Glossary

audition — to try out for a role in a movie, play, or TV show

critics — in entertainment, people whose job is to give their opinions about movies, TV shows, or music

debut — first public appearance

duet — a song that is sung by two people

music chart — list of the most popular songs or albums

premiere — the first public showing of a movie

producers — people who get the money and organize the people to make a movie or TV show

tabloids — newspapers and magazines that focus on stories about celebrities

To Find Out More

Books

Hannah Montana: A Day in the Life
  (Modern Publishing, 2007)

Hannah Montana: Best of Both Worlds Boxed Set
  (Disney Press, 2007)

Hannah Montana: Hannah's Hang-Out Guide
  (Modern Publishing, 2007)

DVDs

*Hannah Montana & Miley Cyrus: Best of Both Worlds
  Concert: The 3-D Movie* (Walt Disney Video, 2008)

Hannah Montana Vol. 1: Livin' the Rock Star Life
  (Walt Disney Video, 2006)

Hannah Montana Vol. 2: Pop Star Profile
  (Walt Disney Video, 2007)

Hannah Montana Vol. 3: Life's What You Make It
  (Walt Disney Video, 2007)

Web Site

tv.disney.go.com/disneychannel/hannahmontana
At the official *Hannah Montana* web site, you can watch
video clips, listen to your favorite songs, or e-mail your
favorite character.

Index

About the Author

Jennifer Magid is a writer and an editor who has worked for MTV, *In Style*, *Teen People*, and Weekly Reader. She has also written for a number of magazines and web sites on everything from health to fashion. Jennifer has lived all over the country, from Oregon to New York. She currently lives in Dallas, Texas, with her dog, Ajax. She dedicates this book to her niece Maddy, who loves reading.